ISABEL
BISHOP

Photograph by Michael Rolston

ISABEL BISHOP

PRINTS AND DRAWINGS • 1925–1964

Designed, printed and distributed for The Brooklyn Museum
by Shorewood Publishers Inc., New York City

Text by
UNA E. JOHNSON
Curator of Prints and Drawings,
The Brooklyn Museum

Research by
JO MILLER
Assistant Curator of Prints and Drawings,
The Brooklyn Museum

Monograph No. 2 in the series:
AMERICAN GRAPHIC ARTISTS OF THE TWENTIETH CENTURY,
published by The Brooklyn Museum under a grant from
The Ford Foundation in Humanities and the Arts

ACKNOWLEDGMENTS

Special acknowledgments are made to the artist Isabel Bishop and her dealer Mr. Alan D. Gruskin, Director of Midtown Galleries; to the Whitney Museum of American Art and The Wadsworth Atheneum; to Mr. Donald A. Bullard for permission to print his untitled poem inspired by an exhibition of Miss Bishop's drawings and prints and to Mr. Thomas B. Hess, Editor of ART NEWS magazine for permission to reprint *Nell Gwyn* by William Carlos Williams; to Mr. and Mrs. Frederick Gash, and to Dr. and Mrs. T. Durland Van Orden for permission to reproduce the Isabel Bishop drawings in their respective collections and to Mr. and Mrs. Walter Fillin for making available the Isabel Bishop prints in their collection.

Isabel Bishop

From her studio window hard by Union Square, Isabel Bishop has, for nearly thirty years, carried on a warm, witty and perceptive love affair with the teaming microcosm that makes up this busy pulsating segment of New York City. In fact, she finds it impossible to work in any other place. Unlike many artists, she works what her neighbors call a "9 to 5 day." Through these years of keen and absorbed observations, she has captured the mysterious beauty of the ordinary—the commonplace—in her drawings, prints and also in her more formal paintings. In her concern with the essentialities of the passing scene, Isabel Bishop has deftly recorded the familiar attitudes and the fleeting moods of the wheeling crowds which surge around this well-worn Square. She has observed those individuals who are intent in getting on to their work and those just as intent on not working at all. Office clerks, shopgirls, indolent ne'er-do-wells and wheedling mendicants, diligent newspaper readers and just as diligent loafers. Union Square itself seems to belong to the working people of New York. The little luxuries—pretzels, sliced coconuts, fruit, candy, popular records, artificial flowers, cheap restaurants and shoddy clothing shops—all abound. Youths and girls, tramps, sidewalk orators, occasional loafers taking the sun, the aged, and small scrambling children—all give to Union Square its loquacious and robust vitality.

The artist, Isabel Bishop is perhaps a perfectionist. No gesture or mood is left unnoticed. Her sharply discerning eye has been trained through years of observation and is free of sentimentality. Hers is not the "slice of life" point of view so prevalent among the earlier artists who make up The Eight (the so-called "Ashcan School"), but rather the seeking out of what might be termed the special aura of an individual character or scene. These scenes have interested her not as vignettes or typical views but as the distillations of movement in space and the mottled effects of light which form the integrating forces of her creative work. All her graphic works, whether in prints or in drawings, are conceived as disciplines for her paintings.

Born in Cincinnati, Ohio, soon after the turn of the century, Isabel Bishop spent her childhood in Detroit. At the age of sixteen she came to New York to enroll in the New York School of Applied Design and two years later transferred to the Art Students League. Here she studied painting under the tutelage of Kenneth Hayes Miller and Guy Pène du Bois. In 1926 she rented a loft at West 14th Street where she set up both studio and living quarters.

In 1934, at the time of her marriage to Dr. Harold Wolff, she leased the studio at Union Square where she has worked for the past three decades. She was elected, in 1941, an Academician of the National Academy of Design and, two years later, became a member of the National Institute of Arts and Letters. A wit remarked that Miss Bishop's appointment to the National Academy took the academic out of academician—once and for all. She has taught painting at the Skowhegan School of Painting and Sculpture and has served on many art juries. In the latter capacity she has shown a rare understanding of other styles of art than her own. Her unprejudiced and prudent eye and her understanding and enthusiasm for the more avant-garde painting has brought her the respect and affection of many artists.

In the early 1930's Isabel Bishop, Raphael Soyer and Reginald Marsh employed the same model, one Walter Broe, who Soyer found one day on 14th Street intently fishing for coins through an iron grating. After some years, those artists who regularly used Walter Broe as their model, held an exhibition with Mr. Broe as the subject. This gentlemen was not only proud to follow his "profession" as a tramp but was also pleased to serve as an artist's model. In an expansive mood he remarked at the time to delighted press reporters: "on the merry-go-round of life, I've got the brass ring." Looking through her sketches Isabel Bishop amusedly observed that "perhaps American bums are our only leisure class." In a more serious vein the art critic Henry McBride once noted: "her people are glad to be alive, and I take it, particularly glad to be New Yorkers." Such titles as *Union Square Man, Girls Sitting in Union Square Fountain, Noon Hour, Encounter, Office Girls, Reaching for Coat Sleeve, Lunch Counter, Strap Hanger, Snack Bar and Soda Fountain,* bespeak the themes of her paintings, drawings and prints. In the drawings depicting girls and a sofa fountain the artist has caught the very essence of the long clucking sound as the last drop of nectar is sucked through the straw into the mouth of a youthful and satisfied consumer.

In 1941, soon after Hayter first established Atelier 17 at the New School for Social Research in New York, Isabel Bishop joined the small group of artists who were diligently working under Hayter's encouragement and his severe demands for fine craftsmanship. Isabel Bishop's interest centered not on the experimentation or exploitation of the possibilities of the intaglio plate but rather on the spatial elements achieved through the clean, spare use of a single line. This deliberate economy of means and the resulting lack of technical flourishes are noted in the etchings and one engraving that presently encompass her intaglio work. Her etchings, small in size and intimate in feeling, preserve, in an era of the large proportion, the exquisite tradition of the "cabinet print."

Although Isabel Bishop would modestly disclaim any such comparison, her prints remind one of those small Old Master prints in which a single figure makes up the complete composition. One may recall the beautifully wrought prints of Rembrandt in which he explored and delicately set down on his copper plate the changing moods and postures of a group of seventeenth-century mendicants. In her extended series of etchings known as the "overcoat series" Isabel Bishop carries a commonplace genre theme of a man taking off his coat or shrugging himself into an overcoat. The artist enjoys the casual manner in which people sit in public squares and lounge on public monuments, and her prints and drawings reveal an informal charm rare in the impersonal environment of a large city.

Isabel Bishop, throughout her years as an artist, has striven for completeness rather than suggestion in her work and assiduously has refined her personal observations and her own expression. Her figures come alive through precisely elegant lines. Her paintings are the final results of hundreds of pen and ink sketches and not a few etchings. She may work for a year on a single subject—carrying it through drawings and prints to the final painting. With pencil, brush or etching tool, Isabel Bishop always seeks to delineate specific forms in space—forms touched with the illusive magic of glowing light.

In the pages which follow appear Isabel Bishop's own thoughtful and personal statements concerning genre drawings and the rendition of the figure in art which stem from the belief that good modern masters share the same ideas as the old and that the academic painter cannot understand or sense the incompatibility of styles. Also included are the poems of two friends, the poets William Carlos Williams and Donald A. Bullard. The pencil and gouache drawing reproduced opposite Dr. Williams' poem *Nell Gwyn* was chosen to accompany his verses. The poem by Donald A. Bullard was composed after the poet had seen an exhibition of Isabel Bishop's paintings and drawings.

UNA E. JOHNSON

TWO PERSONAL ESSAYS BY ISABEL BISHOP

"Isabel Bishop Discusses 'Genre' Drawings"

reprinted from AMERICAN ARTIST, June, 1953

"Genre" drawings are never heroic, never in the "grand manner," and never large. Also they are never "compositions." In them, form and content seem united by magic—or at least by accident.

In the exhibition of French drawings, lately seen at the Metropolitan Museum, there was a small Fragonard depicting two peasants in a "Roll in the Hay" with this quality. It is at once all *life* and all *art*. It has a severe order but looks as casual as a snapshot. It is so sensuously rendered that the peasants breathe and sweat, yet together they make a form as regular as a Greek vase.

In this particular kind of artistic expression the subject must seem unmanipulated—as though a piece of life had been sneaked up on, seized, and somehow became art, without anything having been done to it. This is the way it *seems*, which is part of the content. Goya, Rembrandt, Brouwer, van Ostade, sometimes Dürer, have this quality—also van Gogh, and others, of course, but the list would not be long. Fragonard usually has not this character, I should think. Rembrandt is the only artist of the highest rank to have it. Rubens—who can set a limit to his genius?—nevertheless, he does not have this quality. His drawings are alive to the utmost—but they express life expanded, and thus, in a sense, manipulated. This is true of Raphael, also, and of Michelangelo.

There is a question: If one longed to follow in the footsteps of the "genre" masters, at no matter how great a remove, should one take Goya, Brouwer, van Gogh, or even Rembrandt for a model? Humbly, I think "no." There are reasons why this kind of drawing has to be studied indirectly. For one thing, these drawings have the air of having just barely "come off," of having achieved a form almost fortuitously, as a by-product of the passionate attack upon the subject matter. This makes them hard to learn from. Also, the completeness of submersion of the art-form in the content produces an effect of uniqueness in each instance. How unlike the "grand" drawings, where every example evidently embodies the same great concepts and principles of art!

In Rubens, in Michelangelo, in Raphael, the make of the form is visible. It is possible, for instance, to see a little into the turning of a surface by means of a deepened transition tone next to reflected light; into the use of small dark caves where forms meet and press on each other; to see the desirability of plumpness in the middle of a form and of delicacy in the attenuated parts.

The grand, the heroic draftsmen, then, had better be the models, though one's aim be far from heroic and grand. With their august help one might learn to lay one's traps and spread one's nets, to snare the subject matter of one's own intuition and life experience, however special and small.

"On the basis of Occam's Razor (which is: 'the terms in an argument may not be multiplied except out of necessity'), the revolt against specific subject matter in painting and sculpture, in our period, was necessary—even overdue. And of all subjects (*no* subject may be taken for granted!), the NUDE should be questioned most severely.

Though the undressed model is fun to draw, the requirement of relevance for painting is more strict. Presenting a specific human being in such an unusual position for the general eye, as having no clothes on, brings an extra term to the 'argument,' that is, unless a larger statement is reached.

Traditionally the NUDE was used to express formulations about life as larger-than-life or more perfect-than-life; as Heroic or Ideal. But what shall provide the larger statement when these attitudes are *rejected*—as we do, in fact, reject them! My attempted solution is to try for mobility in the form. When mobility is introduced into a picture, the possibility is expressed that whatever is represented there *can* change its position, though all may be described as still. This communication, which must be made through the total form in the picture (and is quite a different thing from movement), releases the content! Potential for change opens the door to so much. Were mobility achieved, the limitations of the specific subject could be both kept and transcended, nudity becoming a term in the larger theme—no longer an extra term in the 'argument,' or subject to Occam's Razor.

Anyhow, one can try for this!"

Statement by Isabel Bishop for the catalogue,
Contemporary American Painting and Sculpture, 1963,
University of Illinois, Urbana.

POEM WRITTEN ON THE OCCASION OF AN EXHIBITION OF MISS BISHOP'S PAINTINGS AND DRAWINGS

"Grand Central, let 'em out please, watch the doors!"
In His own Image did He make all men.
"One ham on rye, I'll have a coke, what's yours?"
From Adam's side our mother moves again.

"Canarsie, Harlem, Yorktown and the Narrows"
Sing, messenger, above the IRT.
Who gets the breaks, the outrageous slings and arrows?
Is there a voice that calls for her and me?

"Out please, getting out please, getting out!"
All lines are running late—to Heaven and Hell.
Warm smells and lights and bodies gird about;
Redeem, illumine and transfigure all.

Oh! ever young and ageless Mother Eve
Be with us till we take our final leave.

DONALD A. BULLARD

CATALOGUE

NOTES ON THE CATALOGUE

Dimensions are listed in inches with height preceding width. Measurements given for intaglio prints are those of the plate mark; sheet size is given for drawings. Where editions are known, they are listed and range in size from 20 to 40, but never exceed 50. The artist prints her own editions in her studio. Works are listed chronologically and were dated in consultation with the artist. Prints are usually signed in the lower right corner in pencil.

A representative group of drawings is included in the catalogue.

PRINTS

1920-1929

1. NUDE, ca. 1925
   Etching, 6½ x 5⅝

2. NUDE, ca. 1925
   Etching, 10 x 6¾

3. OVER THE WALL, ca. 1927
   Etching, 2½ x 3½

4. YOUTH, ca. 1928
   Also entitled "Tough"
   Etching, 6 x 4

5. AT THE BASE OF THE FLAGPOLE, ca. 1928
   Also entitled "Idle Conversation"
   Etching, 5 x 6

6. LOOKING OVER THE WALL, 1928
   Etching, 5⅞ x 4

7. MAN STANDING, ca. 1929
   Etching, 5⅞ x 4

1930-1939

8. CONVERSATION, ca. 1931
   Etching, 6 x 4

9. TWO MEN STANDING, ca. 1933
   Also entitled "Two Men"
   Etching, 6⅞ x 4⅞

10. WAITING, 1933
    Etching, 5⅞ x 4

11. LAUGHING GIRL, 1934
    Etching, 4⅞ x 3⅞

12. ON THE STREET, 1934
    Etching, 4⅞ x 10¾

13. NOON HOUR, 1935
    Etching, 6⅞ x 4⅞
    Edition: 40

14. GIRLS SITTING IN UNION SQUARE FOUNTAIN, 1936
    Also entitled "School Girls"
    Etching, 5⅞ x 4⅞

15. SHOWING THE SNAPSHOT, ca. 1936
    Etching, 4 x 3

16. LAUGHING HEAD, ca. 1937
    Etching, 4¼ x 3¼
    Edition: 30

17. OFFICE GIRLS, ca. 1938
    Etching, 7⅞ x 4⅞
    Edition: 50

18. LITTLE MAN, ca. 1939
    Etching, 4 x 3

19. ENCOUNTER, 1939
    Etching, 8⅛ x 5½
    Edition: 40

20. UNION SQUARE MAN
Etching, 3⅞ x 2⅞

1940-1949

21. UNTITLED, ca. 1940
Etching, 5⅞ x 4

22. TAKING OFF HER COAT, ca. 1941
Etching, 7½ x 4½

23. REACHING FOR COAT SLEEVE, ca. 1943
Etching, 5⅞ x 4

24. PUTTING ON HER COAT (FRONT VIEW), ca. 1943
Etching, 6 x 3⅞

25. DEPARTURE, ca. 1944
Etching, 5½ x 3½

26. LUNCH COUNTER, ca. 1945
Etching, 7⅜ x 4

27. ICE CREAM CONES No. 1, ca. 1945
Etching, 7½ x 4

28. ICE CREAM CONES No. 2, ca. 1945
Etching, 7½ x 4

29. TIDYING UP, ca. 1946
Etching, 4 x 3

30. MENDING, ca. 1947
Etching, 4⅞ x 3

31. STRAPHANGERS, 1947
Etching, 4⅞ x 3⅛

32. DOUBLE DATE DELAYED, 1948
Also entitled "Entry-E"
Etching, 5 x 3½

33. GIRL WITH A NEWSPAPER, ca. 1949
Etching, 7⅜ x 4⅜

34. CONVERSATION
Engraving, 6⅞ x 4⅞

1950-1959

35. INTERLUDE, ca. 1952
Etching, 7⅜ x 4⅜

36. OUTDOOR SODA COUNTER, ca. 1953
Etching, 6¼ x 4¼

37. TWO GIRLS OUTDOORS, ca. 1958
Etching, 7½ x 4⅞

38. SNACK BAR
Etching, 6⅞ x 4⅜

39. STRAPHANGERS, No. 2
Etching, 4⅞ x 3

1960-1964

40. SUBWAY STATION, ca. 1961
Etching, 12⅞ x 8⅞

41. WALKING IN THE SUBWAY STATION, 1961
Etching and aquatint, 6⅞ x 9¼

42. NUDE, 1961
Etching and aquatint, 3½ x 6

43. IN THE SUBWAY, 1963
Etching, 9½ x 10¼

44. NUDE, 1963
Etching and aquatint, 5 x 7

45. LITTLE NUDE, 1964
Etching and aquatint, 5¾ x 5

DRAWINGS

1929

46. HANDS
Pencil, 8¾ x 6
Signed "Isabel Bishop" in pencil, lower left
Midtown Galleries

1930-1939

47. MEN IN THE PARK, 1933
Pencil, pen and ink, 9 x 8
Not signed
Midtown Galleries

48. MAN IN THOUGHT, ca. 1933
Pen, ink and pencil, 7¾ x 8¾
Not signed
Midtown Galleries

49. NUDE, 1933
Ink and wash
5½ x 3½
Signed "Isabel Bishop"
Collection of Mr. and Mrs. Frederick Gash

50. SLEEPING MAN, ca. 1934
Pencil, pen and ink
10¼ x 8⅜
Signed "Isabel Bishop" in pencil, lower right
Midtown Galleries

51. WAITING, 1935
Ink, wash and pencil
7⅛ x 6
Signed "Isabel Bishop," lower right
Whitney Museum of American Art

52. GINA, 1938
Pencil and pastel
12 x 9
Signed "Isabel Bishop" in red chalk, lower right
The Corcoran Gallery of Art

53. HEAD
Pencil with red crayon and white chalk on buff paper, 11¾ x 8$\frac{3}{16}$
Not signed
The Wadsworth Atheneum

54. SEATED GIRL WITH NEWSPAPER
Ink and wash, 8 x 5
Signed "Isabel Bishop," lower left
Cranbrook Academy of Art

55. TWO GIRLS OUTDOORS
Ink and pencil, 14½ x 10¼
Signed "Isabel Bishop," upper right
Verso: 5 sketches
The Corcoran Gallery of Art

1940-1949

56. LUNCH HOUR, 1940
Ink and wash, 8¼ x 6⅛
Signed "I.B.," lower left
University of Nebraska Art Galleries

57. TWO GIRLS, ca. 1940
Pen, ink, and wash, 17 x 23
Not signed
The Butler Institute of American Art

58. PORTRAIT OF
ABRAHAM WALKOWITZ, 1943
Ink and wash, 13½ x 10¾
Signed "To Abraham Walkowitz–
Isabel Bishop"
The Newark Museum

59. GROUP OF MALE FIGURES,
ca. 1945
Pencil, pen, and ink, 13¼ x 16½
Signed "Isabel Bishop," lower right
Verso: Pen and wash with pencil
drawing of same subject
Not signed
Midtown Galleries

60. MAKE-UP, ca. 1945
Pen and ink, 8¼ x 7
Signed "Isabel Bishop" in pencil,
upper right
Pen and wash sketch of a girl's
head in bottom margin
Verso: Pen sketches of three bending
figures and one seated figure
Midtown Galleries

61. TWO GIRLS AT
LUNCH COUNTER
Ink and wash, 6 x 6¾
Signed "Isabel Bishop," lower left
The Columbus Gallery of Fine Arts

62. GIRL YAWNING
Pen and ink, 6½ x 4
Not signed
Collection of Mr. and Mrs. Alan D.
Gruskin

63. NUDE WITH A TOWEL
Ink and wash, 6½ x 4¾
Not Signed
Mulvane Art Museum

64. WAITING
Ink and wash, 5½ x 4⅛
Signed "Isabel Bishop," lower left
Dallas Museum of Art

65. YAWNING
Pen and ink, 12 x 9½
Signed "Isabel Bishop," lower center
Addison Gallery of American Art,
Phillips Academy

1950-1959

66. ICE CREAM CONES, ca. 1955
Pen and ink with pencil, 11½ x 8½
Signed "Isabel Bishop" in pencil,
lower left
Verso: Ink and wash drawing of two
female figures eating
ice cream cones
Midtown Galleries

67. SKETCH FOR NUDE No. 2,
ca. 1955
Gouache and pencil on masonite,
15 x 14½
Signed "Isabel Bishop" in white
gouache, lower right
Collection of Dr. and Mrs.
T. Durland Van Orden

68. GROUP OF MEN
Pen and pencil, 4¼ x 3½
Signed "Isabel Bishop," lower right
The Wadsworth Atheneum

69. MAKE-UP
Ink and Wash, 8 x 5
Signed "Isabel Bishop," lower right
Addison Gallery of American Art,
Phillips Academy

70. THE POCKET BOOK
Ink and wash, 6¾ x 4⅛
Signed "Isabel Bishop," lower left
The Metropolitan Museum of Art

71. SEATED NUDE
Ink and wash, 7 x 6½
Signed "Isabel Bishop," lower left
Los Angeles County Museum

72. SODA FOUNTAIN
(woman seated facing left)
Pen and ink, 11⅞ x 8½
Signed "Isabel Bishop" in pencil, lower right
The Brooklyn Museum

73. SODA FOUNTAIN
(woman seated facing right)
Pen and ink, 11⅜ x 7⅜
Signed "Isabel Bishop" in pencil, lower left
The Brooklyn Museum

74. TWO GIRLS AT LUNCH COUNTER
Ink and wash, 6 x 6¾
Signed "Isabel Bishop," lower left
The Columbus Gallery of Fine Arts

1960-1963

75. STANDING NUDE, 1963
Pen, ink, and wash, 10½ x 13
Signed "Isabel Bishop"
Verso: three wash drawings of two women
Midtown Galleries

76. GIRL SEATED ON BENCH
Pen, ink, and wash, 8 x 5½
Not signed
Collection of Mr. and Mrs. Alan D. Gruskin

77. STUDY FOR "THE CLUB"
Casein, pencil, and wash, 16½ x 19½
Signed "Isabel Bishop" in pencil, lower right
Collection of the artist

78. STUDY OF SEATED MAN
Ink, 4³⁄₁₆ x 3⁹⁄₁₆
Signed "Isabel Bishop"
Fogg Art Museum, Harvard University

79. STUDY OF SEATED MAN
Pen and ink, 6⁷⁄₁₆ x 3³⁄₁₆
Signed "Isabel Bishop"
Fogg Art Museum, Harvard University

80. TWO GIRLS, ONE ADJUSTING HAT
Pen, ink, and wash, 8⅜ x 4⅝
Not signed
Collection of Mr. and Mrs. Alan D. Gruskin

PLATES

1. NUDE, ca. 1925

2. NUDE, ca. 1925

3. OVER THE WALL, ca. 1927

4. YOUTH, ca. 1928

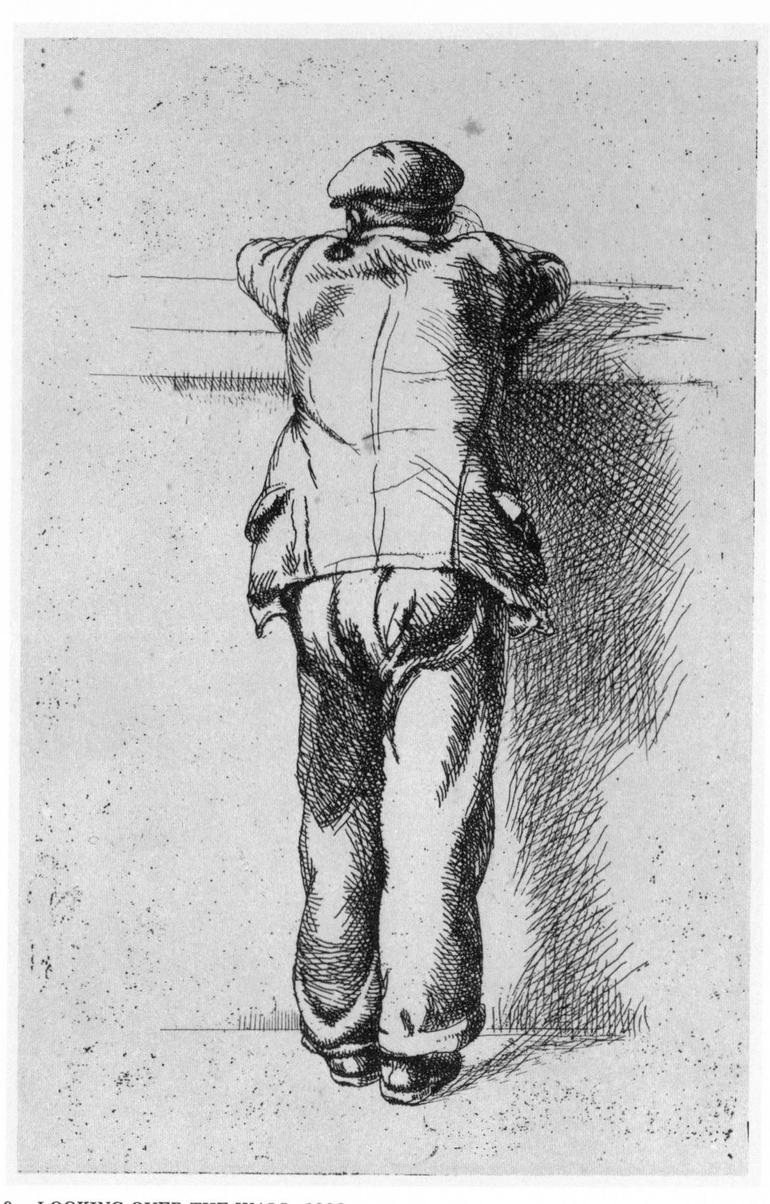

6. LOOKING OVER THE WALL, 1928

7. MAN STANDING, ca. 1929

8. CONVERSATION, ca. 1931

9. TWO MEN STANDING, ca. 1933

12. ON THE STREET, 1934

13. NOON HOUR, 1935

14. GIRLS SITTING IN UNION SQUARE FOUNTAIN, 1936

15. SHOWING THE SNAPSHOT, ca. 1936

16. LAUGHING HEAD, ca. 1937

19. ENCOUNTER, 1939

22. TAKING OFF HER COAT, ca. 1941

23. REACHING FOR COAT SLEEVE, ca. 1943

25. DEPARTURE, ca. 1944

30. MENDING, ca. 1947

32. DOUBLE DATE DELAYED, 1948

33. GIRL WITH A NEWSPAPER, ca. 1949

34. CONVERSATION

37. TWO GIRLS OUTDOORS, ca. 1958

38. SNACK BAR

40. SUBWAY STATION, ca. 1961

41. WALKING IN THE SUBWAY STATION, 1961

42. NUDE, 1961

Poem to accompany
SKETCH FOR A NUDE NO. 2
commissioned by ART NEWS

Nell Gwyn,
it says in the dictionary,
actress

and mistress of Charles the Second:
what a lot
of pious rot there is

surrounding
that
simple statement.

She waked in the morning,
bathed in
the King's bountiful

water
which enveloped her
completely and,

magically
with the grit, took away
all her sins.

It was the King's body
which was served;
the King's boards which

in the evening
she capably trod
she fed

the King's poor
and when she died
left them some

slight moneys
under
certain conditions.

Happy the woman
whose husband makes her
the "King's Whore."

All this you will find
in the dictionary
where it has been

preserved forever
since it is beautiful
and true.

WILLIAM CARLOS WILLIAMS

67. SKETCH FOR NUDE, NO. 2, ca. 1955

43. IN THE SUBWAY, 1963

44. NUDE, 1963

51. WAITING, 1935

53. HEAD

71. SEATED NUDE

72. SODA FOUNTAIN (woman seated facing left)

73. SODA FOUNTAIN (woman seated facing right)

77. STUDY FOR "THE CLUB"

CHRONOLOGY

1902	Born Cincinnati, Ohio. Daughter of Dr. J. Remsen Bishop. Spent childhood in Detroit.
1918	Entered New York School of Applied Design for Women to study illustration.
1920	Transferred to Art Students League of New York to study painting with Kenneth Hayes Miller and Guy Pène du Bois.
1926	Lived and worked in loft at 9 West 14th Street.
1930	Joined Midtown Gallery group.
1934	Married Dr. Harold G. Wolff. Leased her Union Square studio.
1936-37	Appointed instructor at Art Students League.
1938	Commissioned by United States Government to paint mural at New Lexington, Ohio Post Office.
1940	Son born. Elected Associate Member of National Academy of Design. Exhibited at New York World's Fair.
1941	Elected Academician of National Academy of Design. Studied engraving with Stanley William Hayter at New School for Social Research.
1943	Elected Member of the National Institute of Arts and Letters and awarded $1,000 grant.
1946	Elected Vice-President of the National Institute of Arts and Letters. First woman officer since the Institute's founding in 1898.
1956-58	Taught at Skowhegan School of Painting and Sculpture.
1963	Resumed teaching at Skowhegan School.
1964	Continues to work at Union Square studio.

AWARDS AND HONORS

1940 American Society of Etchers, New York City: First Prize.

1943 National Institute of Arts and Letters Grant: $1,000.

1946 Library of Congress 4th National Exhibition of Prints: First Purchase Prize.

1947 American Society of Etchers, New York City: American Artists Group Prize and Noyes Memorial Prize.

ONE-MAN EXHIBITIONS

1932 Midtown Galleries, New York, New York

1936 Midtown Galleries, New York, New York

1939 Midtown Galleries, New York, New York

1940 Herbert Institute, Atlanta, Georgia

1942 Midtown Galleries, New York, New York

1945 Smithsonian Institution, U.S. National Museum, Washington, D.C.

1955 Midtown Galleries, New York, New York

1960 Midtown Galleries, New York, New York

GRAPHIC WORKS IN PUBLIC COLLECTIONS

Addison Gallery of American Art, Phillips Academy, Andover, Massachusetts

Baltimore Museum of Art, Baltimore, Maryland

The Brooklyn Museum, Brooklyn, New York

Brooks Memorial Art Gallery, Memphis, Tennessee

The Butler Institute of American Art, Youngstown, Ohio

The Corcoran Gallery of Art, Washington, D.C.

The Columbus Gallery of Fine Arts, Columbus, Ohio

Cranbrook Academy of Art, Bloomfield Hills, Michigan

Dallas Museum of Art, Dallas, Texas

Fogg Art Museum, Harvard University, Cambridge, Massachusetts

Fort Wayne Art School and Museum, Fort Wayne, Indiana

Los Angeles County Museum, Los Angeles, California

The Metropolitan Museum of Art, New York, New York

Mulvane Art Museum, Topeka, Kansas

Museum of Fine Arts, Boston, Massachusetts

The Newark Museum, Newark, New Jersey

St. Paul Gallery and School of Art, St. Paul, Minnesota

University of Arizona, Tucson, Arizona

University of Nebraska, Lincoln, Nebraska

The Wadsworth Atheneum, Hartford, Connecticut

Whitney Museum of American Art, New York, New York

SELECTED BIBLIOGRAPHY

References given pertain chiefly to the graphic work of the artist and are listed alphabetically by author or title with the exception of exhibition catalogues which are listed under the name of the city in which the gallery is located.

BOOKS AND PERIODICALS

"The Bishop Girl Seen in Drawing Show." Anon. Rev., *Art Digest,* XVI (June, 1942), p. 12, 1 illus.

Breuning, Margaret. "Bishop Show Emphasizes Solidity," *Art Digest,* XXIII (May, 1949), p. 15.

Campbell, Lawrence. "Isabel Bishop," *Art News,* LIV (November, 1955), p. 50, 1 illus.

Craven, Thomas. *A Treasury of American Prints.* New York, 1939, pl. 11, 12, 2 illus.

de Kooning, Elaine. "Isabel Bishop," *Art News,* XLVII (May, 1949), p. 46, 1 illus.

Dennison, George. "Isabel Bishop," *Arts,* XXXIV (May, 1960), p. 58, 1 illus.

Dodgson, Campbell. *Fine Prints of the Year. London,* 1936, pl. 65.

"Drawings by Isabel Bishop." Anon. Rev., *American Artist,* XIII (June, 1949), pp. 49-55, 6 illus.

Harms, Ernest. "Light As The Beginning–The Art of Isabel Bishop," *American Artist,* XXV (February, 1961), pp. 28-36, 60-62, 14 illus.

Hess, Thomas B. "Big Business Taste: The Johnson Collection," *Art News,* LXI (October, 1962), pp. 32, 55-56, 1 illus.

"Isabel Bishop Shows Her New York Types." Anon. Rev., *Art Digest,* X (February 15, 1936), p. 19, 1 illus.

Lane, James W. "Bishop," *Art News,* XLI, (June, 1942), 1 illus.

McBride, Henry. (a column), *New York Sun,* May 22, 1942.

"A Miller Pupil's Shackles Loosen." Anon. Rev., *Art Digest,* X (March 1, 1936), p. 16.

"Poet In The Square." Anon. Rev., *Time,* May 16, 1960.

Reese, Albert. *American Prize Prints of The 20th Century.* New York, 1949, p. 20, 1 illus.

Sawin, Martica. "Isabel Bishop," *Arts,* XXX (November, 1955), p. 50.

Schuyler, James. "Isabel Bishop," *Art News,* LX (May, 1960), p. 14, 1 illus.

Slatkin, Charles E. and Shoolman, Regina. *Treasury of American Drawings.* New York, 1947, pl. 137.

Watson, Forbes. "Isabel Bishop," *Magazine of Art,* XXXII (January, 1939), p. 53-54, 1 illus.

EXHIBITION CATALOGUES

Brooklyn, New York, The Brooklyn Museum. *American Printmaking. 1913-1947,* 1947, introduction by Jean Charlot, p. 20, 1 illus.

Brooklyn, New York, The Brooklyn Museum. *Golden Years of American Drawings 1905-1956,* 1957, text and catalogue by Una E. Johnson, p. 15.

New York, New York, Whitney Museum of American Art. *Second Biennial Exhibition–Part One–Sculpture, Drawings and Prints,* 1936, No. 69, 1 illus.

New York, New York, Midtown Galleries. *Isabel Bishop,* n. d., foreword by Reginald Marsh.

WRITINGS BY ISABEL BISHOP

"Concerning Edges." *Magazine of Art,* XXXVIII (May, 1945), pp. 168-172.

"Isabel Bishop Discusses Genre Drawings." *American Artist,* XVII (Summer, 1953), pp. 46-57.

"Kenneth Hayes Miller." *Magazine of Art,* XLV (April, 1952), pp. 168-169.

COVER: Snack Bar
Catalogue No. 38

DESIGNER: Adele D. Rotkin